Sweet Home,
Saturday Night

Sweet Home, Saturday Night

POEMS BY DAVID BAKER

THE UNIVERSITY OF ARKANSAS PRESS

FAYETTEVILLE   1991

This book was designed by Chiquita Babb using the typeface Galliard.

The paper used in this publication meets the minimum requirements of the
American National Standard for Permanence of Paper for Printed Library
Materials Z39.48-1984. ∞

Library of Congress Cataloging-in-Publication Data

Baker, David, 1954–
    Sweet home, Saturday night : poems / David Baker.
      p.   cm.
    ISBN 1-55728-202-1. — ISBN 1-55728-203-X (pbk.)
    I. Title.
PS3552.A4116S94   1991   90-49609
813' .54—dc20   CIP

ACKNOWLEDGMENTS

My thanks to the editors of the following magazines where these poems first appeared, often in earlier versions: *Chariton Review*: "Demolition Night at the Speedway"; *Crazyhorse*: "Breakdown"; *Indiana Review:* "Formal: A Catalog"; *The Journal*: "Driving Past the Nuclear Plant"; *Kenyon Review*: "Cardinals in Spring," "Generation"; *Missouri Review*: "Confessional: Domestic of Terror," "Pastoral: A Fragment," "Survey: Last Reading"; *New England Review:* "Missouri," "More Rain"; *North American Review*: "Web"; *Poetry*: "Starlight," "Sunbathing," "Supernatural: A History"; *Poetry Northwest*: "Natural: Our August Moon," "Political: Forms of Joy"; *Quarterly West*: "Murder: Crows"; *Shenandoah*: "Patriotics"; *Sidewinder*: "Sentimental: An Epithalamium"; *Southern Review*: "Dixie," "Sweet Home, Saturday Night"; *Western Humanities Review*: "Envoi: Waking after Snow," "November: The End of Myth." "Inside the Covered Bridge Historic Site" first appeared in *Jumping Pond: Poems and Stories from the Ozarks*, edited by Michael Burns and Mark Sanders.

I am grateful to the National Endowment for the Arts and to Denison University for support during the time when many of these poems were written.

CONTENTS

IV. Where We Live

I. Drive Away Sorrow

Lay my head on the railroad line,
Train come along, pacify my mind.

NOVEMBER: THE END OF MYTH

We parked beneath that poor, bending tree.
It was our mistake, all along.
We curled in our friends' mild cabin
cupping the mulled wine, leaning

to taste pears touched
in cinnamon, swaying there content
while the split wood wept and wiled away in its own smoke.
And sometime in those meaningful hours, we

who have never found a use for the thing
except to mismanage its name,
as is our bitter nature, did not hear
the hedge apple at last

let go. It left
a little footprint on our hood.
It rolled beneath the less burdened tree, in that darkness—
not a child's forsaken ball, not the body

of a green, malignant thought, neither omen nor even
punishment for our evening's joy,
though we called it so.
It was a hedge apple, only. It was nothing

we would ever hope to hold, in love or burning thirst,
to our parting lips—we
who mistake such things for signs
and for our sustenance,

we who've simply stayed too long.

STARLIGHT

Tonight I skate on adult ankles across the blue pond
sifted with snow, back and forth across ice lit
as if from underneath by moonlight and many stars.
As I sweep and turn, the wind warms itself
inside my collar and rings the cattle's crystal bells
where they huddle over ranging fields. *Starlight*,
she whispers, *bright stars*, though the tiny
woman I have always loved can't see them.

What is it like to drift between your life and your life?
Needles dot her arms, nurses rub their cotton cloths
like clouds across her face. Like melting ice
the fluids drop down trickling to their tubes.
When I take her hand, and off we go, our skates slice
lightly in the rippled ice, her hair blown-frost
and tangled. She tugs my arm and sings *I wish*.
Brittle tree limbs crackle in sudden gusts

and so she leaves me, skating ahead with surprising grace,
called to by something else. Once I watched her
pile of precious scraps become a quilt.
Once she pulled it to my chin and in my first sickness
I kicked it off. The fragile ice, blue-floured ice
we cut across, groans and gives, grows weaker.
Each time we pass in time. Once she wept when
her child's children, sullen in their hand-me-downs,

scuffed early home from school and wouldn't speak.
In this grown place, across blue sheets, we swing
until my ankles tire and ache. Who can finally reach her
where she whips beneath the trees? She pirouettes and floats,
she spins alone in spray, her body lifting luminous and whole
like song, now like a prayer. So this is what we are.
On she glides when I have stopped. On she sails when I have
laid me down and under starlight closed my eyes.

WEB

Hardly more than a salting
   of frost on a single leaf,
a nest of fog, the web
appeared in the morning light
   in the walnut tree.
I thought it would burn off,

dew in the warming sun. It stayed.
   It grew, though not so
perceptibly day by day—
rather at moments when
   weeks had passed, when I held her
near the window, both of us

startled by the change. "There,
   see how it's grown?"
Yes, she'd say, already going,
yes: though sometimes I
   would stay a little longer:
how the gray-white gauze of web

had spread, a few more leaves
   caught up and curled
brown, the quiet worms at work.
Yes, like summer going.
   Yes, until I could not
bear the dying tree

and so, wrapping pages
    of the unread evening news
and lighting the tip into a torch,
I walked into the yard alone,
    walnuts, old leaves
in the yellow grass,

and raised my arms together,
    awkward candle, raised
myself to touch it. It was gone,
vanished before I knew,
    burned before I burned it
by the fierce, simple

nearness of the flame: *yes*,
taken, like love, before I knew,
    without a touch.

MURDER: CROWS

I can't help it. The brute dawn brings the day.
The window where my coffee's steamed with me
blackly since four, my sleep gnawed open
by a scream, becomes a field, like prophecy.

We'll let her go, he breathed, *we'll see*;
so my blood-gloved neighbor released to the herd
the runted lamb already ruined in the womb.
He is a gentle man, who hopes. His sheep stand

now luminous, fatal as patchfog, huddled
around that shy heart where the fence should be.
I guess they've been that way all night
though only since the dawn has so slowly

beat away the dark have I been able to see
their deadly self-indulgence. He didn't lie.
The clean-cut stumps glow like cellar bulbs.
The field grows long and starved. Silently

a kitchen light labors to cross its backyard, high
with weeds. The dawn bleeds out inevitably.
And so, like negatives of stars reflected,
or like me, the crows begin to stir where they

have landed, attacking the fencerow and baled hay.
They throb among the clover. They hop, wait,
screaming with the certain glee of screaming there.
I see his sheep brood and suffer, shifting about.

I see my nightmare blacken in the broad daylight.

DIXIE

> *Now if you want to drive 'way sorrow,*
> *Come and hear dis song to-morrow.*

> —Daniel Decatur Emmett

for Bob Cantwell

I.

I had no idea.
In Ohio, in a field
near where we've found ourselves
blackhearted and alone,
where the winter-blanched
stalks of corn stubble stand around,
wind rasping through

their ripped sleeves, where
yesterday the whole field seemed
a sad, gray blur
after last week's scum of snow,
the Snowden brothers' twin stones
crumbled and are gone.
Proud relatives, you guessed,

or some high-minded public
servant, must have remembered
the two sons of slaves
just long enough to engrave
and raise one more,
store-bought stone, there
in the backwoods churchyard

where we marched
over the grave-soft earth.
Weak light fell
through the frames of black branches
where no song was.
Only: *They Taught Dixie*
To Dan Emmett.

2.

Braced by snow, but booted hard,
the back door for days locked
tight with ice gave way.
And so help us both, we tramped into
no good single story again, your home.
The logs we lugged in,
the weeping logs we stacked and lit

could barely thaw each other out
to burn. The walls glowed
with their other life, your daughters'
drawings plastered everywhere:
dazzling suns, ruby trees, birds colored
every possibility, summer pictures
like sweet outflung windows

the cruel wind blew into,
frameless as mirrors, back-looking, devastating,
beautiful. Our guitars loved us
the little they could,
two freezing singers whose lives
slept safely somewhere else
in the concurrent dark,

whose songs were stolen.
Isn't that the irony
of misplacement, that we remember ourselves
through others? The whiskey's smolder
faded late and slow. Outside
the sleet crept scraping
among the haggard trees, like a spy.

3.

Uncle Dan in blackface,
Uncle Dan in greatcoat and boots stomping
across the stage-planks, deliberate
in his dirge, a walk-around so pure
with longing and regrets
the audience shuts up and stares:
In Dixie's Land where I was born

Early on one frosty morn,
Look a-way . . . up-state New York, 1859.
It's snowing, how many hundreds
of miles from Ohio
where the Snowden brothers pluck banjos
and sing for passing coaches
from their porch. He's on his way

to being famous, his minstrels
in demand, though today his white ears
crack in ferocious cold. He turns,
spanks and twists his floured hands
high in the air, though
his back seems broken
it's so bent, and now shuffles

to the other side, face colored
into a negative of clown,
singing of mistakes . . . *Look a-way,*
Dixie's Land. Camera powder explodes
and clapping scares a flock
of pigeons from their oak. He watches them
scatter, recollect, fly away.

4.

Snow falls over Ohio.
I have a window so wide
it's like I'm sitting outside, easy chair
kicked back, half-drunk, freezing.
The truth is, I've been trying to write
a love poem all this time
and don't know how. She's gone

and won't come back, next-door neighbor
to your daughters in that fenced-off,
foreign country inside this one.
If I sight them right, along
my thumb, the stumps align
like crumbled, nameless, blackened stones
in a graveyard—but you know that

already. The trees
crowd around gray in their daguerreotype.
It should be spring but snow keeps coming.
There should be flowers
but the stubble field and fencerows
grow only murderous with crows.
Like little pieces

of a poem gone wrong, and torn,
the snow keeps floating down,
and she is gone.
Uncle Dan lived a long time
and I have his words on good authority:
I wish I had never writ
that God-damn song.

5.

How do you tell people
you love them in this cold
country too big for its own good?
So help me, I can't stop
from seeing the children, blood-wild
and eager, trooping across
their families' fields,

the stolen song of another country
gone wrong on their lips.
I can't stop from seeing
the Snowdens starving for a song.
I had no idea
it would turn out like this.
Like some silly, lovely-painted clown,

a bluejay fiddles away right now
in the redbud's heart,
harping on and on outside
my picture window. I look away.
You would say he's full of life, old friend,
and you'd be right. You would say,
in all your hope and sadnesses,

he signals the going-on of things.
And you'd be right again, I'm almost afraid
to think. I see you sitting
in your summer-frozen house, alone,
thumbing a book, breathing into your hands,
and wish the same old wish, that we were
anywhere but here.

II. Breakdown

Oooo,
I'm drivin' my life away.

MISSOURI

1.

This is the living we make. This is our love and pain.
I don't need to tell you the urgency of rainfall when
the rain hasn't touched us for weeks, but the light
skeining the sky through a long run of willows
was so true it could have been prayer spoken low.
It was scattered and slow like heat lightning and silent
as a storm miles away coming. We strained

our small motor to pull harder in the sludge of river turned
stagnant—a scum of eggs and raw foam—from its thirst.
We wanted to gather the last of our lines.
We wanted to come clean on the shore in a cloudburst.
We wanted to listen to the chatter of each dry leaf.
It's important to get this right. A strike of lightning
can kill quicker than drought but we wanted to see it ourselves.

2.

Anything? nothing hanging at the limblines threading the
thick night into cobwebs and old bait

Anything? nothing bitten on the twenty-pound test twine
strung down each limber sapling hammered hard into the cracked
smelling mud

Anything? nothing flaming on the trotline dripping nothing
where the cottonwood roots tangle in the water nothing nosing a
jugline back into another dead eddy

Anything?

Anything? nothing not a drop from the sky not a whiff of wet
wind not one breeze nothing

3.

Not storm, not rain, not wind, not a prayer.
Not the growl of a pickup

                              ranging over the levee road—
but the light kept coming. Not a farmer
working down the low ground to save his runt crop.

Beyond the far, sluggish bend where the sandbar
piled itself to rest, that eerie light

kept flaring up and nearing. Nothing thundered.
Nothing fell but sweat and the last discarded bait.
A deep vibration held the humid night

                                    when we shut
our motor down. The light kept darting out—

until we caught its pattern,
until at last we understood the sweep and motion

4.

of a headlight dogging bank to bank,

and then, around the curve, as if
its beam were winding some snagged thing to shore,

its barges first, slowly the river tug labored
into our night
                —ponderous, black—
like a huge, caught fish wallowing half-

dead. We stared through the snow of bugs' wings
in our lantern light.

We wanted to believe someone could do something right.
But one barge seemed to lean, too close, nose-down—
then a deep, long, disturbing groan
                                said something
is wrong. Then they didn't move again.

5.

When you are lost, when you are tired or terrified,
your voice slips back into its old first place.
It makes the sound your shades make there.
We had heard it in the farmers' aching voices.
We had heard it in the herons' cries and everywhere
their cries came back as ours from the breaking land.
We heard it in the boatmen's cursing fear.

6.

    Listen under the black night under the bass thrum of big
engines churning the tug rocking it under that echo shaking down
the long banks
                                   now
    Listen under the upturning water and risen ancient muds
outflung in urgency under the wild water raking its nails on a near
bank under the sobbing water
                                   now
    Listen under the grind of work under sweat under a deep
vibrant fatigue under the bloodthirsty psalm of the mosquito at
your earlobe under your skin
                                 now
    Listen under your skin

Listen under the oldest voices there aching again in your
language speaking *now* speaking *under* speaking fear and the dying
world falling away

now

7.

Not storm, not rain, not wind—it wouldn't come for weeks.

When the tug tore away, already morning
tipped the low leaves in the willows.

They left the barges rammed into the sandbar.
They knew the river would drop lower
                                        and left their load
to bloat like a carcass,
to stink, to ruin. The night's fine

dew rose as fog and would be gone before the sun
could burn it,

and the tug went on—

past us, where we had cleaned up our things for the night,
past where we had waited with them hours unseen,
hearing the old failure, the pain.

8.

All we wanted was to live by the river.
It's important to get this right. We wanted to listen
to the night's unchanging hum of survival.
We wanted to ease ourselves down the water
and take what had come to us fighting from the dark.
Weeks still the drought would describe itself in
widening mud cracks, in stench, in a hardening, brutal

ache along the shores and fields and in our oldest hymns.
Its heat would drain each body, blanch each leaf,
and when the rains came at last like a balm to soak
the hurt world back, we would still speak as softly
as that—as our shades do, when the river dies under them—

the nets drying and useless on the thick mud banks,
the small figures working all night in their dark.

9.

    Saying This is the living we make. This is our love and pain.

PATRIOTICS

Yesterday a little girl got slapped to death by her daddy,
    out of work, alcoholic, and estranged two towns down river.
America, it's hard to get your attention politely.
    America, the beautiful night is about to blow up

and the cop who brought the man down with a shot to the chops
    is shaking hands, dribbling chaw across his sweaty shirt,
and pointing cars across the courthouse grass to park.
    It's the Big One one more time, July the 4th,

our country's perfect holiday, so direct a metaphor for war
    we shoot off bombs, launch rockets from Drano cans,
spray the streets and neighbors' yards with the machine-gun crack
    of fireworks, with rebel yells and beer. In short, we celebrate.

It's hard to believe. But so help the soul of Thomas Paine,
    the entire county must be here—the acned faces of neglect,
the halter-tops and ties, the bellies, badges, beehives,
    jacked-up cowboy boots, yes, the back-up singers of
    democracy

all gathered to brighten in unambiguous delight
    when we attack the calm and pointless sky. With terrifying
    vigor
the whistle-stop across the river will lob its smaller arsenal
    halfway back again. Some may be moved to tears.

We'll clean up fast, drive home slow, and tomorrow
    get back to work, those of us with jobs, convicting the others
in the back rooms of our courts and malls—yet what
    will be left of that one poor child, veteran of no war

but her family's own? The comfort of a welfare plot,
    a stalk of wilting prayers? Our fathers' dreams come true as
    nightmare.
So the first bomb blasts and echoes through the streets and shrubs:
    red, white, and blue sparks shower down, a plague

of patriotic bugs. Our thousand eyeballs burn aglow like punks.
    America, I'd swear I don't believe in you, but here I am,
and here you are, and here we stand again, agape.

SURVEY: LAST READING

      My father's teaching me
   to map the land, the wild, rock-wretched
      Ozark foothills not an hour's
   drive from his house. I can't see him:
but across the mud-choked gulley, through ivy,

      up a hill gnarled
   with vines, his two legs delicate behind
      the tripod's three so that
   the plumb-bob hangs breathless,
pointing straight to hell, he's got me

      sighted like a dreamy
   animal about to feel the bullet blow
      its life apart. We've been at it
   all day long. I poke around
one last time to locate solid ground, steady

      my ten-foot rod marked
   in red inch-slivers, then slowly,
      so as not to blur his vision, rock it
   back and forth. He needs
to get the highest reading, lightly

      guiding his scope
   until he focuses, shoots, then fixes it
      in his book. *Good!* his echo

bangs. Minutes later he scrambles up
unscratched out of huckleberry brush,

    flops down, sharpening
    his mechanical pencil like a switchblade,
      beginning to subtract. *So what's
    it like?* He means: to teach.
He's anxious for his balding, broken-up,

    doctor son who writes
    poetry. I think of twenty freshmen
      whom I love for fifty minutes
    three times a week at one o'clock,
whom I teach to slice the hide off words until

    they bleed clean,
    digestible, dead. "They'll do,"
      I grin. *What?* He flings a pine cone
    at a squirrel who chirrs, drops
his walnut, claws around to the shade-side

    of his maple tree.
    "Whatever I say." We both know
      better. His figures show we're exactly
    five too many elevenths of an inch
off whack from where we started. I fail

to see the problem.
   But when we track down to the car, loaded
      behind equipment, my feet slip
   wild through the moss, branches slash me,
the clouds I steer by blur and divide

   in the shifting
   sky, and all my mapper's tools
      beat their wings against my chest
   to get away, to fly above this world
too imprecise for anything but art.

SONNETS FROM ONE STATE WEST

1. Inside the Covered Bridge Historic Site

Nothing about this is right. I have torn
my way down the old path, overgrown, thicker

than I had thought with ivy, brush, stickers
as long as safety pins—and all to mourn

a sway-backed bridge, a relic as forlorn
as the bone-dry creek bed strung with liquor

bottles that it spans. No mushroom picker,
squirrel hunter, or arrowhead collector born

with common sense would come out of his way
as far as I have to get here. So much

for history. Getting back out, I know,
will be worse. I see just one of two ways:

to battle the green wall of brush from which
this path has come—

                or there, into which it goes.

2. *Sunbathing*

My neighbor's new store-bought dog yaps again,
hungry, crazy with heat, maybe both,
stretching his short chain until he chokes.
The little dab of sunshine I lay down in
has drifted away, into the shrubs,
but I'm not budging. *I'm surely dying!*
my cruel neighbor's pup keeps yelping

and, so help me, I suppose he is,
his poor dog's life ticking away like my own.
I guess I'll stay right here in the cool shade
and let him cry for us both—our sad,
single bodies, our chains and our bones,
all burning down to ash and grime
quickly enough on their own sweet time.

3. Driving Past the Nuclear Plant

How often have you heard it: tornado
rips through trailer court leaving dozens dead,
homes demolished. Shoot of straw burrows
into pine fence post. Or: family killed,
dog found barking on the roof.
                              So last night
as the rain rattled off my hood like rocks,
I looked, and there, black in the few hundred feet
between storm clouds and ground, the twister dropped.

I pulled over, cut the engine, covered
my head to wait it out.
                              But no wind roared.
The rain let up. When I looked once more,
only the reactor's tower funneled
in the dark. I left. I drove so fast
I swear I rose, swirling in the window's blast.

MORE RAIN

1.

This is all still something of a mystery.

In 1953, just after that war,
my Uncle Wayne took a wooden bootjack and whacked
my father, just once, upside his head

—to whip him
into shape,

he said.

2.

Shape for what? nobody really figured out,
or still won't say.
I was born about a year
later.

I believe
it was raining hard
when Wayne belted my father—as
it is now, again, for the umpteenth time
this drenched, green, madly

growing spring.
My father bled like a stuck pig,
to use their favorite way of recapturing the moment.

3.

Whenever the rains keep coming down floating
as they do now in the morning
in just enough cool June stillness to meet themselves
sneaking back up a foot or so
as fog,

and whenever the two sweet gum trees
stationed by my study window
bow so heavy

with the accumulate rains and their own strange,
bobbing, light green seed pods
—which seem, now that I think about it,
like those tiny
floating naval mines, spiked, deadly—
I like to think I understand the whole thing.

4.

What whole thing?

5.

My father will show you, if you ask in the right tone of
    voice,
the long, ragged scar just
under his right ear

and ranging like a map line
down the negotiable border of his jaw.

And in the rain especially,
and the humidity, it will stand out red, still burning.

6.

He was already married, just home from the war: hero.
And he needed, to Wayne, to be whipped.

How Wayne knew this, nobody knows.

But I guess now it's got
more than a little to do with the rains—
the easy rain shaking the grasses,
the rain slipping over everywhere from the rooftops and
    gutters,
the same rain, bad rain,

the constant rain soaking down the roots
until each rotted leaf lets go, pale and conquered,
the rain everywhere,

all the rain hissing and tapping and clouding the day,

the rain,
which has fallen much too much this spring,

7.

and can drive you so crazy
you'll do just about anything

to kill it.

DEMOLITION NIGHT AT THE SPEEDWAY

no cover charge

Reamed as our county may be
from his thirty years' perfect thievery,
the judge has granted his own old Cadillac
a public trial and death. Among rebuilt bombs
and junkers revved to screaming in a field
foreclosed by asphalt track, it's got no more chance
to ride this out unscarred than we do.
Junebugs butt their heads against the lights above us,
crackling like popcorn, blowing out everywhere
in showers of gnatty dust. So
when the starter's flag swoops down,

our one free night explodes, bleachers swoon and cars
careen in gangs, crunching and back-tracking,
ramming up a storm of dust. We rise choking back
our daily agonies of farms in hock, of cousins
locked in crime. We hop in our best threadbare
clothes' last legs to cheer our neighbors
clobbering themselves crazy for the bumpercrop of cash
the judge himself has promised to kick in.
Tonight our entertainment's perfect with a vengeance.
We know these self-same wrecks and shrieks
can't keep this up for long.

BREAKDOWN

Ansted, West Virginia, may be almost heaven
if you believe in songs. It's almost hell, I imagine,
when you choke down coal smoke on your way to work.
But this afternoon where I have sat in winter sun

with a flat six-pack and all my shiny tools,
broken-down between the Lovers' Leap Baptist Church
and one vast rock painted *Welcome!* in sky-blue,
it has all the signs of home. I should have known

when my rattletrap Malibu started nagging this morning.
It coughed from its rusted-out depths up hills
godforsaken, barely eking down. Warning lights
winked like bloodshot eyes too long behind a wheel,

Let this be a sign! Between breakneck curves
and tiny shoulders fogging off to nowhere,
I couldn't stop until something snapped, twanging
like a banjo string, and I coasted into town.

People seem to like me here. They pass nodding
or wave from pickups as I bang and smoke and wave
among the mess I've made. Two young locals
stopped an hour ago to share a beer, and together

we watched a woman wreathe her door with Christmas joy.
When they walked away, they walked away in love,

hands slipped inside each other's flat back pocket.
I have done worse, today, diving and crawling

these unforgiving hills from a hateful house
and classrooms full of someone's bitter children.
But I'm working now, covered, nearly blessed
by the good dirt of Ansted, West Virginia.

Just down the street an artisan has filled his yard
with birdbaths, ceramic tubs, vases, posing
deer stunned perfectly in stone. Above the clutter
he has raised a sign which all this afternoon

I have come to love, *POTERY,* printed in a careful hand.
Reversal, deletion, I don't care. The spirit
of the art lives, as surely as the Santa
lightly reining over the Church's manger scene.

When at last I kick my sockets away, my bolts
and pipes, my empty cans, they make a sort of song.
And when my engine pops, then dies, then chugs,
it catches hold and runs! If I stay, I might do well

to put all my training to good use. I see the sign
I'd paint: *Mechanic School. Learn Grease & Earn Cash.*
I've owed myself a line like that for years.
But the sun of Ansted, West Virginia, is easing down,

and evening sprinkles coal dust on the roofs
where families eat. I sit in my torn plush bucket
and scan the radio, crush a can, accompanied
by the faint bluegrass static native in this range,

gun my engine, punch the brights. The deer stand
frozen, calm. The road, I know, will tangle
up the hills, no fences or signs to steer me straight.
The radio fades from the draining lights

so I strain to catch the gospel group choiring out
their song. *Your loves may strike you down,*
they harmonize to break your heart, *but we know one
who'll come in time, who'll raise you from this ground. . . .*

III. Sweet Home, Saturday Night

It was one mile over
And two miles back . . .

Yeah, yeah, yeah, yeah,
It happened just that way.

SWEET HOME, SATURDAY NIGHT

> *Does your conscience bother you?*
> *Tell the truth.*
>
> —Lynyrd Skynyrd

1. Intro

TURN IT and this fast
the tinny P.A. pops twice, squealing into feedback
so hot and nasty, by the time the singer hits
UP! someone's longneck Stag has stumbled
across a speaker cabinet

and nose-dived off, smacking
the dance floor with a splash—it sprays
like a Roman candle fizzling,
a buck's-worth of beer foam blinking out
in the web of colored X-mas bulbs

strung along the tacky stage for footlights.
The guitars grind out, the bass
kicks in with a shot to the heart . . .
and the lewd wall-clock has fingered itself
five seconds forward.

It's Saturday night at the Com-On-Inn.

2. First Verse

Welcome, grins the stud
lead singer to his crowd,
    to the evening's last set!

He snaps his fingers, in heaven, yanks back
    the mike stand like he's going
to eat it, and

            BIG WHEELS
keep on TUR Ning! he belts out,
    distorting, as the dance floor

fills. They love this song
    —who can blame them?—
all the county's little wheels and weekend

    cowpokes cut loose again
from dictaphones and dreamy bottom lines
    to *Get DOWN!* as one liquid-hipped

woman suggests to the nearest man at hand, who boogies
    across the sticky floor behind her,
crouches, and bellows

                    Par-DEE!
with such surprised conviction,
    you might think he's just come up

with the concept: everybody
    seems to agree. Already the band's
blocked out by the throng

    of jeans and flashy satin
cowgirl shirts and polyester tights.
    But the voice is still there, and the pounding

drums, and the ashtrays begin to vibrate
    on their greasy tables with the buzz
and electric pulse of the music,

    Carry me home to see
my kin! The spotlight cuts through
    the beery air like a sponge.

        (two-guitar vamp, harmony)

    (We should not confuse poetry with rhetoric,
        During the last break the bouncer had to bust
    the art of persuasion. A poem may well use
        up a bad fight between two bikers. *Fuck YOU,*
    the elements of rhetoric, but will subordinate

AND your mother here, AND the horse you rode in
them to its affective unfolding: the right
    on, he said, almost sweetly, stepping between the
true mark of its being a poem and not a piece
    pair. Things got quiet fast. They were not
of discourse. It moves, we have seen, by
    thinking *Obscenity: the root that attaches us most*
association and other subjective resonances,
    deeply to our homeland. They were staring at his
and also melodically.
    baseball bat. *Now MOVE!* he said. And they moved.)

3. Second Verse

No matter where you're sitting,
we've got a little problem,
    don't we? I'm here, and now—where things happen

fast!—you're here. But where is here?
    The *here* where the dancers are
is Saturday, August 15, 1977, ten till twelve,

    at the Com-On-Inn, Rt. 63, Missouri:
and they've obviously all been here
    for hours, well-oiled, half-

tanked or more, and hitting
   on each other like linebackers:
they're fine.

              But already I can't
see the band clearly
   from my solitary corner table

since the dancers took over the floor.
   I can't hear the lyrics
for the static whine, the stomping boots and hollers,

   the garbled intonations—though
the back-up singers' high-pitched
   harmonies, inarticulate, somehow

in sync, keep the song together,
   Oooo Oooo Oooo . . . and you,
of course, can't see or hear anything right now

   but me. The secret,
I'm hoping, must be getting our timing down better,
   not unlike:

             1) the way the singers
   can hold and move *their* song
by sound, by pulse, simple-minded but agreed-on

patterns they've practiced long and hard,
where words are mostly excuses to continue
   the rhythm—who cares,

for instance, among these shoulder-shaking
   secretaries and grease-monkeys, that
I heard old Neil put it down . . .

   if that's even what the lead singer
just growled out?—
                        or 2) the way the musicians

blend into one song their various
   means of counting,
2 beats, 4 beats, depending

   on each player's way of hearing
and each instrument's technical possibilities—
   the bass drum's footpedal double-pumping

the alternating quarter notes, the snare
   popping at each off-beat,
the guitars and bass driving together

   on the background melody, the high-
hat counting time like a ballpeen
   hammer on glass . . .

or 3) the way
the dancers seem so
totally convinced of all of this, this

power, this rhetorically sexual
concoction of ruckus and rhythm, of rock-and-roll
and country/swing, so given over

to it all, so like those two
lovers spooning in their dark corner
where they've been lip-locked and buckle-to-buckle

since the last set's last
slow song, four legs pressed into two,
so convinced of love and beauty, so lost,

so right, so *moved*
by the simple song into *one* place,
one body. Can you see them?

Do you hear it? Are you ready
to let yourself go
a little farther? *Oooo Oooo Oooo* . . .

4. *Chorus and Solo*

Baby, says a wind-swept blonde, atwirl near an amp.
The whole floor's clapping now, hands high
like a mob of children learning jumping jacks,
facing the band who've just hit the chorus.
They always love this part. *Sweet Home, Al-uh-BAM-uh!*

The walls move back. The blonde smooches *Baby* again.
She's looking at the lead guitar player
who's looking dead at her.
I can't stop what's about to happen. So help me.
I guess I'm just dissatisfied with the old standards . . .

she's looking right at *me.* And she's not.
I am, and am not, that guitar player, and these are and are not
my friends and partners and paying customers.
I am sitting here watching myself
sitting at a beer-slopped table watching myself

finger my Gretsch's frets and stare at a blonde babe
(please, try to understand these times)
who's staring back mouthing *Baby baby baby!*
This is/was my band. I can't help what's about to happen.
Lord I'm coming home to you . . .

Hell, son, you've GOT to pay attention, and the heel of Bill McMillan's out-of-date Beatle boot cracks down on the slender, scuffed slats of the second-floor floor over Shaw Music. *You've got to listen, you've got to count. Move your right foot up and down, like this.* He pounds out eight beats of nothing but beats. I'm nine and this lesson is only halfway over. 7:15. My fingers have been bleeding all week. I want to play it, I want to do this well, but I can't seem to get the time quite right: ten fingers and two hands and one foot, each moving at a different time: one song. One song. *You've got to count it out . . .*

One, two, three, four, four twenty-two. There you are, dear. That's $4.22 change back, Lula. You come back soon. And with such simple authority my grandmother completes another transaction at the J.C. Penney fabric counter. I love to watch her. I love to run my hands along the bright materials and shake the thimble drawer like her register full of money. I love to stack high the wooden spools of thread, and when I give her my sore hands, she says *Sore hands make a strong heart,* and shows me again her pin-swollen fingers and her calluses gray as nickles. *See, baby?* And when another order comes zipping down from the upper offices, through the singing air, I think it's like an arrow in a slow war: but it's really a piece of paper clothes-pinned to a metal wire. The lady up there slings it down, my grandmother catches it. Words with more work to do. A song. *Zzzzz* in the air. . .

Z Z Z Z I cut into the lean side of the elm tree. I'm Zorro in my stocking cap and my black cape and my broom-handle. I signify myself first into the tulip bed, then the sandbox sand, now the rough grass which slices off like a flattop with each touch of my name, *ZZZ*. I can make one in three moves. *Over, down, over. One, two, three . . .*

> *One, two, three, four. Done. Did I do it right this time? Did you like it?*

> *(two-guitar vamp, harmony)*

> *(He thought what they said had merit, and*
>> The truth is, *sometimes I think I'm several,*
> *what they felt was serious. Deferring to*
>> sometimes *I, myself* seems merely provisional,
> *his slaves' opinion did not deprive him*
>> much less a solo voice than an improvised chorus
> *of authority or power. It was schoolteacher*
>> of concurrent influences. All I need, I confess,
> *who taught them otherwise. A truth that*
>> is a handful of lines, a wah-wah to run together
> *waved like a scarecrow in rye: they were*
>> the hot notes, and a little stage. I'm here, now,
> *only Sweet Home men at Sweet Home.*
>> hoping you understand, *shifting from foot to foot.)*

5. *Third Verse*

   In Birmingham they love
the Guv-nuh! Dennis is up-stage
   again, tilting his mike like a star

sipping a shoe of champagne, Mark and Tim
   are jamming together
on the bass and guitar

   background line, and Roxanne drives down
on the high-hat, rocking on her seat
   like a truck ride over gravel:

and I've stepped back
   into the semi-dark side of the bandstand,
sweating like a pig as I punch

   off the fuzz footpedal, surprised
at my solo, amazed at the crap
   I get away with—

                        old lines memorized,
   scales cut into pieces, bent
strings picked to scream like hot cats—disappointed

again with my imagination. Cut loose
from the pattern of back-up,
    given any freedom to play any notes, I seem drawn

to the ready conventions,
    out of fear, to establish
some authority: my solo was all hype, stolen

    licks, cheap fingerings—childhood,
grandmother, nostalgia, you know—
    all the usual moves

strung together in a dried-up stream
    of self-consciousness, all
the usual moves, out of fear of sounding foolish.

    And they lapped it up
like free beer. *Now we all did
    what we could do!* At least we're cooking hard together,

the place is *rockin',*
    it's *gettin' DOWN,*
the song itself tight as a fist. *One*

    body. Like a physical force,
the blast from the amps and speakers again dictates
    the very pulse of my heartbeat

and so I let it: *one pulse*: I let the anonymous
    power of volume and beat
drive its icepick through my eyes,

    I let the song
play itself with my hands, touch itself
    with a single finger

until it screams: the dancers
    are out of their heads,
twirling, hustling,

    flirting
with the selfless images of themselves
    on the mirrored wall,

wild. *Does your conscience
    bother you? Tell the truth!*
When the strobe light kicks on, igniting

    the room, exploding
again and again, it's like we're all characters
    in a slapstick newsreel, ghosts

against a wall,
    notes on a burning page.

6. Chorus and Solo

Are you with me? *Sweet Home, Al-uh-BAM-UH!*
Sing it! We're back at the chorus.
Even the stragglers at their lone tables are clapping
and hooting along. And when the blonde
rocks around again, it's clear she's waiting no longer:

she wants me for being up here: I want her to.
We can't help what's about to happen. She smiles.
She slices open her mouth with her slow, long tongue and licks
her own hand. She stares at the body of my guitar.
Baby, she breathes. *Sweet Home, Al-uh-BAM-UH!*

I've slipped my glass slide onto my left fourth finger
and ease it down my neck—an obscene gesture whining out
its obscene scream of feedback. *Can you beat that?*
She throws back her head, clutches her thighs
with both hands, and rides the swirling air

like a goddess, hunching the song itself.
I run the slide up and down my neck, faster.
Lord I'm comin'—and she's not waiting, she's
on the floor, she's wet with beer dripping
off her sudden nipples, lit by ecstatic lights,

the sheen of her skin an exotic fruit's: she cranes
back in a semi-circle of dancers, riding

her orgy in love with the crowd's loud love of her,
then hops up again: she looks at me, she licks her thumb,
tests her rump for fire, and *One hour, baby,* she kisses—

home to you! But I'm getting ahead of myself:

*Not even nature can
change its narrative flow.* I decide this at the last break, chomping my
cup of ice, picking my dark way down to the creek out back of the bar
where I surface for air and the singular buzz of quiet. *Nature's not
narrative at all,* I hear my voice say, a faraway ringing in my ears. On a
flat stretch of gravel and sand, humped in the bare moonlight, a small
pile of mussel shells, pried open, picked apart, cleaned out, dried. They
might have been here for a hundred years or an afternoon. There is no
way for us to know. But they are here now, the *here* we've settled on,
and no sneaky coon, no pair of scavenger crows, no night-hidden
creature who may have dined on the sloppy mess is here at the *here*
we're sharing, the *here* of our lyrical intersection. *The truth is,* chimes
the poet, *there is no story, there is only the wanting to tell.* And so that's
true enough. The clay bank above my right shoulder erodes only as we
try to imagine it as it was yesterday, or a year ago, in contrast to its
present state of being merely *bank.* Now, here, it is only here: or not,
depending on your view. *The truth is,* harmonizes the poet, *the others
there with us will not understand why we are as we are with no cause
visible, no object hanging overhead, no fear like the past, present. . . .* The
truth is, to tell a story requires two wholly unnatural impositions: time
(a fiction) and timing (a fictional device). It is 1977 and it is 1988 and so
time passes. It is even 1999, if I say so, and so I do. Say it or not. But

the tension between the times—the possible erosions of actions and peoples, memories, eons, mistakes, the changing dramatic settings—gives us our story. And to make a story good, like every stand-up joker knows, requires a right sense of timing. *Tell the truth,* one bum says. *Why?* comes the reply. *It never hears me.* Release the punch line at the right moment. It's a matter of counting: one, two, three. . . . *Truth is what,* laments the hapless lover, *must be delayed but not denied.* With so many choices, truth becomes harmonic, *polyphonic,* a texture of voices, a chord, song, a fabrication not unlike a grandmother's quilt. *The truth is, there is no story, there is only the wanting to tell.* To which the song itself replies, *Tell the truth.* The moonlight, the shells, the grimy water. *Nothing happens except as a simultaneous phenomenon of being.* The shells, the moon, the one voice: the shells.

　　　　(two-guitar vamp, harmony)

　　(I hate to hear the beat of my heart;
　　　　Get me the FUCK out of here! Now. Please,
　　it is a relentless reminder that the
　　　　Baby? She's got him cornered and he loves
　　minutes of my life are numbered . . . .
　　　　it. He says, *Give me four good reasons why*
　　A received idea: that the genius of rhythm
　　　　I should take you home. Okay, one, and she
　　is expressed through noisy, emphatic
　　　　smiles, *Sweetie, I hate this dump, it's so . . .*
　　regularity. False. The tedious rhythmic

fake. Two: I hate these people. They're always
primitivism of rock: the heart's beat is
primitivism of rock: the heart's beat is
　　　here. It's Sooo boring. Three, she's got her index
amplified so that man can never for a
　　　finger stuck at an obscene, precise angle in his
moment forget his march toward death.
　　　bellybutton, *I HATE this goddamn song. Four:)*

7. Fourth Verse

Oooo Oooo Oooo . . .
They love this song
　　—who *can* blame them?—so when

I step back still hot, still pumped up
　　from my second solo,
when the whole band

　　detonates at last
into the final verse—two guitars and bass
　　throbbing together, Roxanne's drums

pressing like power-drills,
　　Dennis beside himself, perfectly *on*—
the dancers have given themselves

completely over
to the song: greased with sweated-
    out beer, their shirts

aflame, scorched with the passionate impulse
    of bodies for bodies, *Lord*
they get me off

    Sooo much! it's as if
they have been here
    forever (*in amber? in crystal?*) in a blasted

ritual describing what
    will persist should the world
of this evening ever end: their story's

    become
their rhythm: like some posthistoric
    tribe, they seem to reinvent themselves

and the very expression
    of their sensational delights
with each mutation of steps. Can you imagine

    the marquee outside next week?—
Saturday, August 22,
    the Com-On-Inn Features the Latest Craze,

"Cotton-Eyed Joe
    Meets The Bump!" It's exotic, comic, real
as the hybrid monsters of a discount drive-in flick . . .

    and it's all I can do to keep up
with them: I can only play, so I
    play: for the grace

of their good dancing,
    for the dozens of them jamming in time
on the tiny floor—rocker and hick—

    for the smoke of their cigarettes
hanging out radiant and cool, a half-life
    devolving above them, for

the lights, for
    their beautiful debris,
for the casual abandonment of conventional

    gestures, for each transformation
of impulse, each misstep, each fall,
    each spontaneous movement

and seamy result: I play.
    They pick me up when I'm feeling
blue! Now how 'bout you?

8. Chorus (repeat, with guitar)

We slam into the final chorus like a wreck.
On each hard down-beat, Dennis leaps
into the frantic air: *SWEET HOME AL(uh) BAM(uh)* pounds
like a monstrous pulse, an incredible, chuffing clock.
Tim's driven to one knee, ear plastered

to his amp, shooting-up feedback, blinded with it.
The dancers rant back *Sweet Home Al-uh-BAM-uh*
crazy as killer cheerleaders in love
with their love of our love of this song
that's become pure noise and played-out passions.

The truth is, it's time we got this thing over with.
It's ground my fingers down bad to the bone.

But the dancers are slapping their hands together,
screaming back *Turn it up!* and *Don't stop!* and smearing
their heels into spilled beer and stomped butts,

wild with our song. The truth: it's far too late
for anything else and we all know it.
The real lovers are long gone to their private
rooms and truck-beds *Oooo Oooo Oooo*
and I am looking past the pain, past the lights,

past the writhing dancers, through the wreaking
contagion of the liquored-up air,
at the man far in the back who's been sitting alone
all night. I grip a chord change. He's trying to levitate
out of his chair. *SWEET* None of us can help it:

•

(*To confront the dominant discourse it has been necessary*
where we are is where we are, *this* song, *this* body.
One truth is, we love it here anyway *HOME*
on the excruciating stage of spent energy and headaches.
If you're still here, you know that
for a painful fact—*à la BAM*—and you *Are* still here

to try to advance on all fronts at once. Inevitably,
—for which, thanks. I vamp down to G, plucking and teasing
a note so loud and high it will ignite
for your lyrical pleasure *UHH!* and for the dancers,
and for the storyless (*do* you believe that?) man wobbling now shell-
shocked past his table and stumbling toward the opening

this strategy has meant resources have been overstretched . . .
door where the long night's smoke streams out
into the imaginary dark. *Where the skies are* we all
harmonize *so BLUE!* The dancers keep throbbing
and sweating, *One more* stomping *time!* and *Turn it up!*
so that the whole floor quakes and the footlights

it has accepted that no text is ever closed, none is ever
pulse *AL-UH* heart attack. *Lord I'm comin'*
stuck as we are between rock and an unreal rollercoaster
of words no one can hear for the noise. *BAMA*
The man stops by the bar, nodding around
and the dancers *We Love You* and the dancers—

    more than provisional, including this one now ending . . .)
Lord I'm comin' home—and they are pleading *Don't*
Stop Turn it up! They are facing us, grinning like the dead,
One more they are chanting *TIME Turn it up*
they are all looking *Don't stop* up here *Play* they are
We Love you! screaming *BABY* screaming *SWEET! TURN IT*

9. Coda

So we do.

IV. Where We Live

When you get home, baby,
Write me a few of your lines.

GENERATION

imagining a son

As if the wind warns *shhh* in the evening willows,
two young redwings rinsing in the clear creek
abandon their joy and sleek away, sudden
as each other's shadows in the low, light-shot leaves.
Already the shallow water settles back and burns.
Already you could be older than I was scouting
for bait from the weed-bank with my father.

Do you see? There, on the creek's other side,
last glow under the sun-gone bank, a few minnows
cruise away and then hold, slivers, bare fingerlings,
as if signs of crawdads slick among bottom stones,
bait-sized perch urging back in a tangle of roots.
Everything knows I am here. Everything hides.
Once the silver moon hung its hook out

in lantern-light. It was only an hour from now.
He set dozens of lines along the trackless river.
He cupped a match and breathed into the black, dry wood.
He slipped hooks through the spines of tiny fish
and tossed them in, their tails sizzling away
from the lamp in my hand. If I thought we could
catch some, if I thought, tugging off boots,

rolling jeans to our knees, we could wade in
and lift the seine between us like one unfurled hand,
we would lug them sloshing in buckets down

to the river where the creek slips in and goes.
Already dusk has seeped away from the black-lit limbs.
Already an owl curses back at the sky, answering
to nothing, whining its self-starved wish.

Can you hear me? This is not about becoming a man,
but becoming. Maybe the crickets sang all night.
Maybe the shadowless bats remembered the cry of their young.
I want you to love that because you could.
Maybe we caught a fish, if it mattered, but we walked
for hours through his one, unconditional night,
and he carried me all the way back. Son,

everything knows I am here and is hiding.
I know your shadow roosts in the trees I imagine.
Let it tear free, and come hunt me down. Let me go on,
if I must, in its grip. Already I slip through the creek
just to touch these bodies, to burn them on my hooks,
just to see whose shape even now might strike,
blazing out of this fatherless, poetic dark.

WHERE WE LIVE

for Ann

1. Sentimental: An Epithalamium

Our willow lets its limbs down
almost to the water, almost so they brush
    the surface sheen, lightly,

    leaf-shadows
the shape of perch, palm-sized, blue-black,
    finning themselves still

    near the shoreline;
and when I touch my heel to the cool
    water and come in,

    you are there, as if always
we have waited for this moment
    when we enter

    each other's outstretched arms,
wade together to the center of the small pond
    which has become, now,

    somehow, as we drift together
in the clear sky of water, as perfect as any
    world we could desire—

insects spin in the air,
redwings loosen from the limbs
   of willows, flying

   in small flocks to nowhere
and always returning—shy, miraculous
   acts of grace,

   wind rocking barely
in the blue-black leaves—all
   of this, for hours, clear on the pond

   until, eyes closed,
shaken in and out of the water's own
   arms, we sense these finally

   no longer, feeling
only the pulse of the pond's deepest
   currents, fern

   and water-weeds sweeping
our legs, the soft, prescient muds bearing us
   toward each other, then away;

   so when, at last,
we open our eyes and sunlight has slipped
   from the surface, the redwings

vanished as minnows
in the low leaf-shadow, we let ourselves,
   lazy with love, float

   beneath our willow
once again, whose thin limbs seem always
   to have been waiting for this,

   reaching its tender arms
down to us who are reaching up
   out of the last
            swirling light.

2. *Pastoral: A Fragment*

Where we live, where each green day
blooms early in the born-again trees, lucent with dew
—night-fog sheering away in the first shine—
and so, loosed from its folds, spreads its crawlers out
across our cup-shaped acre of yard
and catches hold,

and where, by and by,
our neighbor's old bell cow wobbles out of her dark-
long drowse to shake herself free
of dust and gnats, her burden of debris, and heads back
into the timothy fields, among cat-calls
and a smatter of crows,

and the first truck bangs its way down
the dirt back road
toward town,

where even the bucket-colored
bird dog no one will claim yips awake at our door step
and wheels again—self-wound and punctual—
instantly out of his head with chipmunks and jaybirds
and hunger, and the grackles go on stuffing
straw down our drainpipes and gutters,

where we choose, all the same,
to turn and live with these placid, ruminant beasts
and rambunctious creatures, where their
myriad sounds revive, and a salvation of light, so early,
where the world yet breathes deeply,
and the green days grow,

and our work does become, again and again, a blessing,
a visible affection,
a matter of love. . . .

3. Confessional: Domestic of Terror

Who was I talking to? Even the barest dark breeze,
easy out there in the stripped-down elms and dingy cedars,
hits the screen door and seethes. It sounds like hunger.
It could be rain. It could be a whole day's slipped away
with nothing to show but a window bruised by drizzle
and a year's black dust. How strange to speak myself
awake to find the room the same, and light
the hollow same, the same low terror simmering like gas
in the left-behind kitchen and ticking in the sink's burnt pans.
How easily could all this ruin be the replicant rain?

She came in the dark and in darkness is gone. When
did she go? That's what the clock asks now blinking its inchoate
digits, counting its pulse from an obvious outage of power.
That's what the clothes say humped in neglect, and the sheets
steeped like old snow or blown sand or simply like sheets
grainy and stained with the casual diseases, the comforts
of lovers. I tell you we stepped out of our lives.
She knelt in the dark by the window and glowed from inside
where I was. She held me for free and again. She lived for a time
in my skin and somehow tore loose, like a shearing

of silk, her ravenous fingers kissing my memory away.
She must have touched nothing, touching my face as she left.

Not until now did I know. Has a whole day passed in this dark?
That's what the wind says between its wiry teeth, and the tires
sizzling outside in the rain like fire or soft cloth slowly
ripping in two. What will I do if she doesn't come back?
The sudden cat stiffens at the dumbcane and purrs
where she's just shredded the season's one paling shoot.
The rage for death was never stronger in her eyes, nor a hunger
for cruelty, nor love. Who else could I tell this to?

And what if she does?

4. Supernatural: A History

Heat and haze. The granular frayed-ends of late night
—the half-light of late afternoon, nearly evening—
and the dead center of a summer field. Heat-waves and dust.
Dust-haze. So the filthy leaves burnish like broken-in leather,
oily from a distance, and deepen when a breeze hits.

The percussive wood-crack—boys and girls run in the heat-waves,
wading, in a drift, as if underwater, through nothing
but more humid air. From where I stand petrified but happy,
holding a bat and starting to take my cuts,
this play of light has much to do with the way the scene

occurs: a figure on first, a figure, now, held at second—
too few of us to fill the necessary field. And *ghost
runner on third!* a voice cracks, calling at my back
when I turn squinting outward into the cream sky.
This could be either memory or metaphor, you understand—

we are as close to love as we've ever been. Field-chatter.
A batter's breeze. All I have to imagine—
across the diamond's thistle and late steam, and dust-motes
like delicate sand afloat, and a distraction of nerves—
is what's already here, filling in for an absence

and particularized at will. A training ground for romantics.
So the boy with the bruised face knocks a bubble
of sweat off his lip, glaring at me, and begins his wind-up.
Desire can be this clarifying—down twenty-five years
and some fifty feet of heat-shimmer and loneliness,

light now like a lotion, a hazy presence at third becomes
a real runner, because we've wished it so—a run, if I'm lucky
enough to hit the pitch wobbling at me like a feather.
But there is one more thing. I'm looking down the line
as I swing—as far back now as my life goes—where the base still

blurs in the gray-white whirl. A ghost. A dazzle of white.
—Or the white-noise of what I've always wanted.—
Until it's you, of course, in the utterly breathless heat.
You, dug-in and grinning, as I swing—at this moment
when the field itself dissolves into tiny, abstract zeroes

and a backwash of vaporous light.
                                        Just like it's always been.
Heat and haze. You. Waving. Beginning to run this way.

5. Formal: A Catalog

Stippled with sweat and singing
   to leaf-bud and bare stem
alike, each in its turn,
thyme   all morning you have tended
   our scatter of herbs
and now catch me lazy

with a fondness of my own.
   I love to watch you
kneel to the tiniest hope
lemon-balm   of green, dabbing water
   to these up-curling lips or pruning
a sore. Together, in spring,

we tracked the tedious migration
   of shade, then charted
and laid-out our plot—
sage   digging and sifting,
   stretching twine between
stakes, planting our bundles of starters

and patting down mounds.
   Now you lean back and smile.
Lines of bright markers shimmer
savory   like a graphic design—

and though this garden may be far
from a catalog's glossy finish,

though a few leaves
    have already been chewed into lace
and others seem handsome
with eggs, though even our hands
    bear the jaundice and scars
of earth, and we could never survive

rue

on our pitiful lot alone, together
    we are nearing a place
where work transplants worry,
where planning blooms
    into patience
and care. I love the way

shepherd's-purse

you love your labor, digging
    again, and sure—our small, straight plants
delicate with sun. You scuff
 your trowel like a pencil. You prod
    and spoon. You poke your fingers
back down into earth,

lovage

so we go on
    singing row after row after row. . . .

6. *Political: Forms of Joy*

So sure of himself, in the simple, soothing way
the very powerful can wave off trouble, or the way the weak-
minded will gladden with form, repeating any pattern,
our cross-street neighbor's challenged child of twenty-two
lifts his auburn arm to wave us home, as he has
every afternoon this sultry summer, and holds it there.

What does he mean today? Is he happy to see us or simply
happy, perched on his curb, clean teeth and T-shirt?
What does it mean that he sits so crookedly, now as always
so awkward, one leg thrust into the gutter, weight on his
barely balancing other hand, or that his surprising muscles
seem forever flexed from the unbidden tension

in his body's attitude to wave? Clearly he is glad.
He's our block's sweet and spiteless angel, our attendant joy.
The only time we've ever seen him cry, last spring,
he'd sneaked behind our fence to watch our weekend chores
and when I crossed beneath the apple tree, raging with my mower,
and raised our mother robin from her nest to scream

and flit and dive, he lifted his wail up with hers
and wouldn't be consoled. How could we tell him her hatred
was pure, even beautiful, born simply of her misunderstanding
of our need to work, and that we meant no harm?

We took him in for water and a tissue. On the news the
    president
kept brushing off questions with a wave, winging it when

he couldn't respond. Reporters edged him in. On TV's
perfect grass, protestors raised their signs and throbbing
    fists.
We watched with him and talked until the robin returned
to nestle among her shadows as we knew she would,
a creature doomed to habit. We walked him home, we
    stroked
his tightened arm, and there he sits so happy now

to see us that we honk, wave back. Sure enough,
as every afternoon this summer, his upheld hand twists
to a fist, and with the precise, fatal aim of the slow-minded
or the so obscenely powerful, like he's seen and learned,
one crooked finger slashing through the fruitful air,
he flips us off with his own peculiar bird. It makes him
    glad.

7. *Natural: Our August Moon*

How these blue hours bless us and keep us
easy in our cushions and comfortable chair, unaccustomed
as we are to peace, to calm, the clarifying dark
smoothing out like a bruise on August's beaten body.
It's been so hot these days the dogs can't scratch.
It's been so bad the razor grass gets sharper
until its blades burn down in little singes and scruff.
I love you more than I could ever tell you,
though language is full of suggestions:

now, while your head lolls in my lap, lightly,
and your shoulders soften with the talcum of sleep,
not a breath stirs the fern at the window, not a breeze,
only the muted, underwater blue of the TV
trying to sell back my soul, all self-love and loathing.
But sometimes, when I hold still enough, you reach
from the regions of sleepers and whisper a moment
the nonsense I love, soft twitters
like sparrows sipping, or a sigh,

or whole landscapes of jabber in phrases so clear
I think you are singing. I want to go where
you've gone to lie so purely at peace.
Not a cloud has passed over, it seems, for hours.
I want to join you like that and speak without guile

or my requisite irony. I'm ready to believe
the heat will withdraw its cruelty, and the neighborhood
listen. I want the ridiculous keys to fall asleep
in their locks and the money in drawers

and on loan to count itself back and forgive,
I'm ready for the dust to wheel and wag
in slow circles away and away, for the crescent moon
to hit its pure high C and hold that note,
like crystal through crystalline leaves.
I love you more than language can hope to explain:
so hum your psalm of sleep-talk and ease, let the grass
swell blue in the lunatic night, I want you
to know I understand. I'll be there soon.

CARDINALS IN SPRING

after Whitman

1.

Tens of thousands on the wing, perennial in April
—think how pure we are now, in retrospect—
tens of thousands in our red caps wheeling down
from Davenport, St. Charles, from Boonville by the river,
from our populous sadnesses driven,

from our seedy backyards driven,
from the bullies and yahoos and doddering folk
of our neighborhoods driven to reclaim
our rightful seats, St. Louis, Busch Stadium, 1968, the same
as '67, as '66, and the season's first pitch.

2.

I don't deny this whole thing
is designed to celebrate our most common desires:
it's spring, we want to win, things grow, we feel
inside ourselves the power of something so immense and primitive
it spreads out unchecked, ritual. *Redbirds!* we sing

as they take the field, uniforms like shiny hieroglyphs,
and scatter across the Astroturf, a sun-lit plain of green stuff
hopefully forever so green, our latest synthesis
of industry, imagination, and the persistent pastoral archetype.
We're all here, never more perfect than now . . .

3.

Brock of the basepath, never more perfect than now,
Javier of the hopping grounder, never quicker,
Flood in his field, and Shannon, and Maxvill at short,
McCarver-in-a-crouch, and suddenly Gibby
whipping his warm-ups in from the natural dirt of the mound . . .

Mom with her bag of fried chicken, Dad with his cooler,
Dad with his scorecard and program, my brother next to him,
Uncle Buster crowding down who yesterday flipped
a knuckler behind his back so powerfully
it arched through an upstairs window . . . never more perfect than
   now.

4.

What is it? I wonder, and Buster brings his arm up to me.
We're all in our red, at last in our row,
Green Level, Section 6, and everywhere the fragrance
of hotdogs and beer, the press of bodies, the voices of thousands
like us chattering, communally wild. *O what is it?*

and now Buster opens his hand, his pure-white present,
and everyone is applauding in one body,
and the sun flames down, and the pressbox glasses over, adazzle,
and I am jumping; and now I think it must be
the icy chiseled heart of winter melting in his outheld palm,

5.

it is the incredible; and now I think
it is the pure/seamy duality of rewritten lives crossing, forever
stitched in red, the yin and yang of postmodern expression,
and nothing less; and now the hatching egg of hope;
and he looks at me, and now I think it is

an antique opaque eyeball, a foggy crystal ball
through which even cliché transcends itself and so signifies
our inarticulate, collective excitement that nothing
in particular, always already, is happening with sensational urgency
. . . and now he's giving it to me. . . .

6.

But how can I know that? How can I say all that?
How can I be 13 and 33 at once, cursed and blessed, crying
with all the fever and joy of the stupid
who know the truth and can't speak it, yet speaking,   *here* . . .
he's giving it to me, and I hold it, *a baseball*

signed by the entire team! I know it: *This is mine
to love!* the whole weighty globe of it, the tens of thousands
in our companionable nest, even the other team loping afield . . .
whoever they are, my own affections having blurred,
for a moment, all the individual images. . . .

7.

When we stand, as we must, when the silence
and fragrant calm settle over us all, as surely they must,
and the caps come off and our hands flutter up
to our felt hearts, when we begin to sing
in a voice so singular it redoubles, echoing off the sky,

we stretch ourselves proud and pulsing, and the music,
like an organic truth, throbs through our veins and temples,
and over the land of the free, *over the vendors and hawkers,*
over athletes and umps, the fireworks blossom
into smoke-puffs and thunder like the storms of creation.

8.

The moment before its beak breaks through the tender shell,
doesn't the fledgling struggle for its whole species,
doesn't its becoming, at that moment, signify freedom and flight,
doesn't longing belong to the family of hope?
And when we sit back trembling and rapt with anticipation,

don't we personify our teeming, human compulsions?
Yet how can we say these things in real life?
All in the space of a moment, between silence and screaming,
between breath and breath, suspended in the nether-sphere
of original joy, aren't we, in each other, renewed?

9.

O thousands of us, tens of thousands with our souvenirs
and our statistics committed to memory where all things
change for the better, we are the bodies of one desire.
And now Gibby, across the semi-precious green diamond,
across the dumbstruck years, stares in for his sign, turns,

and hurtles the first pitch forth, winging it outward,
and we are leaping up, mouthing our first word *O,*
and the ball leaves his whipped arm, and hangs there, for
    us all,
for this moment, this beginning, where we see it still,
all of us, *O!* never more perfect than now.

ENVOI: WAKING AFTER SNOW

When did we drift into each other's arms?
Snow, blue as morning, shakes down
in the branches, not a breath among them.
I can't tell if we're one body or two.
As soon as he's settled, the redbird puffs up
his whole heart to the cold. Don't move.

NOTES

Epigraphs

The epigraph for the first section is taken from a work song in Toni Morrison's *Beloved*. The epigraph for the second section is from a song, "Drivin' My Life Away," written and recorded by Eddie Rabbitt. The third section's epigraph is from Roger Miller's song, "It Happened Just That Way." The epigraph for the fourth section is from Fred McDowell's song "Write Me a Few of Your Lines," recorded by Bonnie Raitt.

•

"Dixie"

Born and buried in Mt. Vernon, Ohio, and still locally referred to as Uncle Dan, Daniel Decatur Emmett is credited with the authorship of "Dixie" in 1858 or 1859. Emmett was a white traveling musician of some fame and little monetary success who often performed as a blackface minstrel, dressing, playing, dancing as a slave. Later in his life he regretted having written this song; far different from its evolution into the rousing, march-paced Southern fight song, his "Dixie" was a walk-around, a slow and somber field song.

The story is further complicated by the possibility that the song, or at least the melody, was passed to Emmett as a young man by two black musicians, Ben and Lou Snowden, also of Mt. Vernon. Composing songs, for Emmett, usually meant writing new lyrics to old melodies—fiddle tunes, field songs, tavern rounds, hymns. Even the single reconstructed headstone of the Snowden brothers supports this theory; their only epitaph reads "They Taught Dixie To Dan Emmett." The song, it seems, keeps changing colors to suit the purposes of its singers.

This poem is dedicated to and spoken to Bob Cantwell—neighbor, writer, musician, folklorist, teacher—who shared this story and his songs with me during a hard time.